D.I.Y. MAKE IT HAPPEN

TRAINING COURSE

VIRGINIA LOH-HAGAN

45th Parallel Press

Published in the United States of America by Cherry Lake Publishing
Ann Arbor, Michigan
www.cherrylakepublishing.com

Reading Adviser: Marla Conn MS, Ed., Literacy specialist, Read-Ability, Inc.
Book Designer: Felicia Macheske

Photo Credits: © Pavel1964/Shutterstock.com, cover, 1; © diogoppr/Shutterstock.com, cover, 1; 3 © Ultrashock/Shutterstock.com, 3; © Rob Marmion/Shutterstock.com, 5; © stockyimages/Shutterstock.com, 7; © txking/Shutterstock.com, 9; © Martynova Anna/Shutterstock.com, 10; © keantian/Shutterstock.com, 11; © Matthias G. Ziegler/Shutterstock.com, 12; © Maridav/Shutterstock.com, 14; © Gustavo Frazao/Shutterstock.com, 15; © Flashon Studio/Shutterstock.com, 17; © View Apart/Shutterstock.com, 18; © MyImages - Micha/Shutterstock.com, 19; © Monkey Business Images/Shutterstock.com, 20; © AllAnd/Shutterstock.com, 21; © Poprotskiy Alexey/Shutterstock.com, 23; © Anteromite/Shutterstock.com, 25, 31; © bikeriderlondon/Shutterstock.com, 26; © Ahturner/Shutterstock.com, 27; © Daxiao Productions/Shutterstock.com, 28; © Matthias G. Ziegler/Shutterstock.com, 30; © Ruslan Kudrin/Shutterstock.com, 31; © wavebreakmedia/Shutterstock.com, back cover; © Dora Zett/Shutterstock.com, back cover

Graphic Elements: © IreneArt/Shutterstock.com, 4, 8; © pashabo/Shutterstock.com, 6; © axako/Shutterstock.com, 7; © Katya Bogina/Shutterstock.com, 11, 19; © Belausava Volha/Shutterstock.com, 12, 20 ; © Nik Merkulov/Shutterstock.com, 13; © Sasha Nazim/Shutterstock.com 15, 22; © Ya Tshey/Shutterstock.com, 16, 25; © kubais/Shutterstock.com, 17; © Fandorina Liza/Shutterstock.com, 19; © AllAnd/Shutterstock.com, 21; © Infomages/Shutterstock.com, 24; © Ursa Major/Shutterstock.com, 26, 29; © LHF Graphics/Shutterstock.com, 29; © Art'nLera/Shutterstock.com, back cover

45th Parallel Press is an imprint of Cherry Lake Publishing.

Library of Congress Cataloging-in-Publication Data

Names: Loh-Hagan, Virginia.
Title: Training course / by Virginia Loh-Hagan.
Description: Ann Arbor : Cherry Lake Publishing, [2016] I Series: D.I.Y. Make
   It Happen I Includes bibliographical references and index.
Identifiers: LCCN 2016004583I ISBN 9781634711043 (hardcover) I ISBN
   9781634712033 (pdf) I ISBN 9781634713023 (paperback) I ISBN 9781634714013 (ebook)
Subjects: LCSH: Obstacle racing—Training—Juvenile literature. I
   Exercise—Juvenile literature.
Classification: LCC GV1067 .L65 2016 I DDC 796.42/6—dc23
LC record available at http://lccn.loc.gov/2016004583

Cherry Lake Publishing would like to acknowledge the work of The Partnership for 21st Century Skills.
Please visit www.p21.org for more information.

Printed in the United States of America
Corporate Graphics Inc.

ABOUT THE AUTHOR

Dr. Virginia Loh-Hagan is an author, university professor, former classroom teacher, and curriculum designer. The only training course she wants to do is one that involves food. She lives in San Diego with her very tall husband and very naughty dogs. To learn more about her, visit www.virginialoh.com.

TABLE OF CONTENTS

CHAPTER ONE

WHAT DOES IT MEAN TO CREATE A TRAINING COURSE?

Do you love running? Do you love jumping? Do you love crawling? Do you love climbing? Then create a training course. It's the right project for you!

Some people train. They train their bodies. They get their bodies ready. They get in shape. They work out. They do training courses.

Training courses are programs. They make people **exercise**. Exercise is **physical** activity. Physical refers to the body. It's about keeping fit. Training courses make people stronger. More training means more strength.

Talk to personal fitness trainers. Get their advice.

KNOW THE LINGO

Burn: pain felt in muscles after training

Carbo load: to eat a lot of pasta or bread before training

Clock time: the amount of time from start to finish

Core: trunk of the body like the stomach and back muscles

Crunches: sit-ups

Gym rats: people who work out at the gym a lot

OCR: "obstacle course race"

PR: "personal record," personal goals

Pumping iron: lifting weights

Reps: repeating an exercise

Ripped: having big muscles

Slip slops: destroyed shoes after a training course

Split: the time it takes to run a specified distance

Tough Mudder: very difficult mud run that requires participants to swim through ice or carry logs up steep hills

Training courses are hard. They're more than just running. They can be **obstacle** courses. Obstacles are things. They make training more fun. People go over obstacles. They crawl through them. They climb them. They make training courses more difficult.

A **course** is a path. Training courses have a starting place. They have a finishing place. People participate. They find their way through. They deal with obstacles. They're timed.

Create a training course whenever you want. You'll break a sweat. You'll get your heart rate up. The best part is getting healthy.

Learn about bodies and muscles.

CHAPTER TWO

WHAT DO YOU NEED TO CREATE A TRAINING COURSE?

Decide the purpose. People like training courses. There are different reasons for this.

➡ **They build physical strength.**

➡ **They build mental strength. Mental means the mind. Training makes people smarter. People solve problems. Obstacles are problems.**

➡ **They prepare bodies. They help people train for bigger events.**

➡ **They make people feel better.**

➡ **They're fun. They can be a party game.**

Consider creating a mud run. Mud runs are extreme obstacle courses.

➡ **Have people work as teams.**

➡ **Have them swim through mud pits.**

➡ **Have them crawl through mud tunnels.**

➡ **Have fun getting muddy!**

Use mud to make things slippery. This makes training harder.

Include obstacles.

➡ **Include a running path.**

➡ **Include hurdles. Hurdles are things to jump over.**

➡ **Include ditches. Ditches are holes. People jump into them. People jump out of them. People crawl in them.**

➡ **Include walls. They're for climbing.**

➡ **Include balance beams.**

Use a gym for indoor training courses.

Decide a **location**. Location is a place. Most training courses are outdoors. Some places have obstacles. You'll have to bring in obstacles to other places.

➡ **Consider playgrounds. They have monkey bars. They have slides. They have balance beams. They have sand.**

➡ **Consider parks. They have benches. They have open areas. They have sports areas.**

➡ **Consider large backyards.**

Check the location.

➡ **Look for slopes. You don't want people to fall.**

➡ **Look for holes. You don't want people to trip.**

➡ **Get permission. Make sure you're allowed to be there.**

Get gear. Things are needed for the training course.

➡ **Get things to make obstacles. Get ropes. Get tires.**

➡ **Get weights. People carry these things.**

➡ **Get timers. Time the participants.**

➡ **Get signs. Mark each obstacle.**

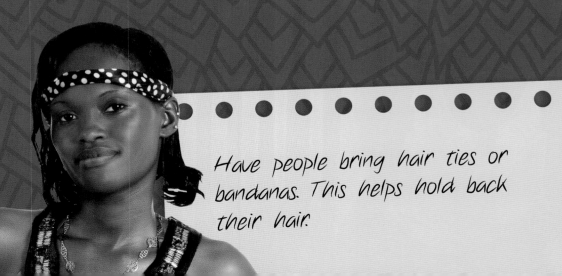

Have people bring hair ties or bandanas. This helps hold back their hair.

TRY THIS!

Create a crazy clothing obstacle course! Have people put on clothes after each obstacle. This'll be fun. This'll be different.

You'll need: articles of clothing, training course, obstacles.

Steps

1 **Create a training course. Create several obstacles. Place an item of clothing at each obstacle.**

2 **Have people crawl under a table. Have them grab a necktie. Have them put on the tie.**

3 **Have people do 20 jumping jacks. Have them grab a shirt. Have them button up the shirt.**

4 **Have people walk a balance beam. Have them grab pants. Have them put on the pants.**

Make sure people have gear.

- → **They need good shoes. Shoes need grip. They need to be light. They shouldn't hold water.**

- → **They need tight clothes. This avoids snags.**

- → **They might need gloves. This prevents rope burn.**

Have people sign contracts. They should not participate if they're sick.

Make sure everyone is safe.

➡ Get **first aid** training. People may fall. They may get hurt. First aid helps with cuts. It helps with scrapes. It works until medical help comes.

➡ Get a first aid kit. It has bandages. It has healing creams. It has cleaners.

➡ Get **emergency** training. An emergency is when something dangerous happens. An example is breaking bones.

➡ Hire a medical person. Examples are doctors or nurses. Make sure someone is there.

➡ Get **spotters**. These people help break falls. They should be at each obstacle.

CHAPTER THREE

HOW DO YOU SET UP A TRAINING COURSE?

Mark the training course.

⇨ Create a path.

⇨ Create a map. Make sure people know where to go.

⇨ Make signs. Include instructions. Make sure people know what to do.

⇨ Tie balloons to the signs. Write numbers on the balloons. Mark the order of each obstacle.

⇨ Test the course. Do this ahead of time. Check to be sure everything works.

Advice from the Field
REBECCA GOLIAN

Rebecca Golian is a personal trainer. She creates exercise programs. She's an obstacle course racer. She works at The Sports Center at Chelsea Piers. She started its first Obstacle Course Race Training Program. She prepares athletes for training courses. She includes exercises that are similar to the training course. She advises, "It's best to prepare your body for anything, as race organizers are constantly changing the courses and adding new obstacles." She suggests training two to three days a week. She prepares people for scaling walls. She suggests doing pull-ups. She suggests doing hanging knee raises. This helps with rope climbs. She said, "Focus an extra day each week to work on your weaknesses."

Stay prepared and organized.

Create **intervals**. Intervals mean different exercises. They're done in a short amount of time.

➡ **Include high-intensity workouts. Intensity refers to activity levels. High-intensity activities pump up heart rates. They require a lot of energy. Examples are sprinting and jumping.**

➡ **Include low-intensity activities. An example is walking.**

➡ **Include rest breaks.**

Create different events. Events make up the training course. They're the obstacles.

➡ Include moving activities. Make people run. Make them jump. Make them do **zombie crawls**. This means they lay facedown. They use their upper bodies. They crawl.

➡ Include activities that build strength. Make people carry heavy things. Make them do pull-ups. Make them do sit-ups.

➡ Include rope climbs. Use a wall. Throw ropes over the wall. Tie thick knots in the rope. This is for people to hold on to. Have people climb up the wall. Have them go over the wall.

➡ Include tire courses. Use tires. Lay two lines of tires. Put them side by side. Have people run through them. Have them put a foot in each tire.

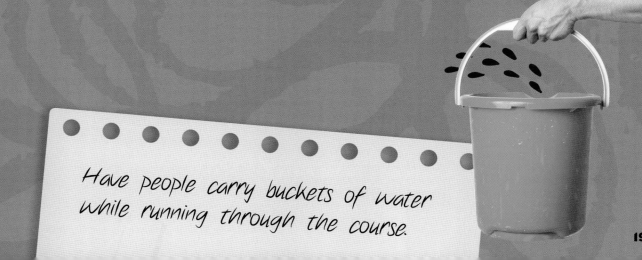

Have people carry buckets of water while running through the course.

Think about how long each event should take.

Create **aid stations**. They're special centers. They provide help.

➡ Set up tables. Set one up at the starting place. Set one up at the finishing place. Set one up along the course.

➡ Get helpers. Have them work at each station.

➡ Provide snacks.

➡ Provide drinks. People sweat. They lose water in their bodies. They need water. Water keeps them from cramping up.

➡ Have first aid kits ready.

Create a schedule.

➡ Decide how long the training course should last. Some training courses are races.

➡ List the starting time.

➡ List the finishing time.

CHAPTER FOUR

HOW DO YOU RUN A TRAINING COURSE?

Greet people.

➡ **Welcome everyone.**

➡ **Get names. Get addresses. Get phone numbers. Ask who should be called in case of emergencies.**

➡ **Give out schedules.**

➡ **Give out maps.**

➡ **Explain rules.**

Have people do **warm-ups**. These are exercises. They warm up the body. They loosen tight muscles. They prevent injuries.

➡ **Stretch muscles. Reach high. Reach past toes.**

➡ **Walk. Jog. Do easy runs. Get bodies moving. But don't do too much.**

➡ **Warm up for 5 to 20 minutes.**

➡ **Slowly raise heart rates.**

Make sure people understand potential dangers.

QUICK TIPS

- Have people walk on cans. Use large coffee cans. Attach straps to each can. This'll test their balance.

- Use hula hoops. They can be used instead of tires.

- Attach bells to hula hoops. Hang them. Have people climb through them. Don't let them ring the bells.

- Make a rope swing. Use a wading pool. Tie rope to a tree over the pool. Have people run. Then, they swing across.

- Give people three sheets of newspaper. Have them place one beneath each step they take. Make tricky turns in the course.

- Host a spaghetti dinner before the training course.

- Use streamers. Create a maze in an aisle. Have people go through without stepping on streamers.

Start the training course.

➡ **Place spotters at each obstacle.**

➡ **Make sure people know about aid stations.**

➡ **Make sure people finish the training course. Make sure they go in order.**

➡ **Assign helpers to be timers. They time each person. They record these times. Place timers at the last obstacle.**

➡ **Consider placing people into groups. Have groups start at different times. Space groups 30 minutes apart. Keep track of each person if you're timing.**

➡ **Consider making videos. Some people may argue about times. They may argue about performance. Videos give proof. They help solve arguments.**

Make the first obstacle easy.

Consider yoga. Yoga consists of different poses.

Have people **cool down**. These are exercises. Bodies are heated. Muscles are hot. They've been working hard. Don't suddenly stop moving. This does harm to bodies. Cooling down is good for the body.

➡ **Loosen muscles. Slowly jog. Walk. Bring down heart rates. Safely return to resting level. Get bodies back to normal.**

➡ **Stretch legs. Stretch arms. Stretch stomach muscles.**

➡ **Shake body parts. Kick. Wiggle.**

➡ **Take deep breaths.**

➡ **Drink water.**

Host a special meeting. Get **feedback**.
Feedback is tips.

➡ **Let people share stories.**

➡ **Ask people what they liked. Find out what went well.**

➡ **Ask people what they didn't like. Find out how to improve. Make the training course better.**

➡ **Ask people for new ideas.**

Give out prizes. Award people for their work.

➡ **Award the best time. This person completed the course. This person had the fastest time.**

➡ **Award the best performer at each event.**

➡ **Award the best attitude.**

➡ **Thank all your helpers. Give them a small gift.**

➡ **Thank everyone for coming. Tell them to come to your next training course.**

Have people run the course in reverse.

D.I.Y. EXAMPLE!

STEPS	EXAMPLES
Purpose	◆ To increase physical fitness ◆ To raise money for the school's athletic programs
Fees	◆ Charge entry fees of $10 per person
Location	◆ School's gym
When	◆ Saturday morning
Schedule	◆ Registration ◆ Warm-up exercises ◆ Events/obstacles ◆ Cooling down exercises ◆ Award ceremony

STEPS	EXAMPLES
Obstacles and events for training course	<ul><li>**Hurdles:** Place hurdles at each corner. Place them on the track. Have people sprint around the track. Have them jump the hurdles.</li><li>**Balancing Beam:** Have people walk across a balance beam. Have them hold a gallon of water in each hand. Make sure to place mats under the beams.</li><li>**Zombie Crawls:** Get open boxes. Place them in a path. Tape them to the floor. Have people do zombie crawls. Have them crawl through the boxes.</li><li>**Circle Hop:** Get pool noodles. Connect the ends. Connect the circles together. Connect them in two rows. Tape them to the floor. Have people hop through each circle.</li></ul>

GLOSSARY

aid stations (AYD STAY-shuhnz) special centers that provide snacks, drinks, and first aid

cool down (KOOL DOUN) do exercises that bring bodies back to resting after high-intensity activities

course (KORS) a path

ditches (DICH-iz) holes or trenches

emergency (ih-MUR-juhn-see) when something dangerous happens

exercise (EK-sur-size) do physical activity

feedback (FEED-bak) tips or advice to get better at something

first aid (FURST AYD) helping to heal cuts and scrapes before medical help can be provided

hurdles (HUR-duhlz) things to jump over

intensity (in-TEN-sih-tee) level of activity

intervals (IN-tur-vuhlz) different exercises done in a short amount of time

location (loh-KAY-shuhn) place

mental (MEN-tuhl) related to the mind

obstacle (AHB-stuh-kuhl) something that gets in people's way

permission (pur-MISH-uhn) consent

physical (FIZ-ih-kuhl) related to the body

spotters (SPAHT-urz) people who help protect athletes by breaking their falls

warm-ups (WORM-ups) exercises that warm up bodies to do high-intensity activities

zombie crawls (ZAHM-bee KRAWLZ) popular move in which people lay facedown and use their upper bodies to crawl

INDEX

LEARN MORE

BOOKS

Dicker, Katie. *Exercise*. Mankato, MN: Amicus, 2011.

Schlachter, Margaret. *Obstacle Race Training: How to Beat Any Course, Compete Like a Champion and Change Your Life*. Rutland, VT: Tuttle Publishing, 2014.

WEB SITES

American Sports and Fitness Association: www.americansportandfitness.com

Obstacle Racing Association: www.obstacleusa.com